IMPROMPTU SPEAKING

10 Strategies to Think on Your Feet
Without Tripping Over Your Tongue

DIANE WINDINGLAND

Copyright © 2022 Diane Windingland

All rights reserved.

ISBN: 9798439796106

Toastmasters International® and all other Toastmasters International trademarks and copyrights are the sole property of Toastmasters International. This book is the opinion of the author and is independent of Toastmasters International. It is not authorized by, endorsed by, sponsored by, affiliated with, or otherwise approved by Toastmasters International.

For My Friends, Family, Clients,
Fellow Toastmasters, and Speakers

IMPROMPTU SPEAKING

10 Strategies to Think on Your Feet Without Tripping Over Your Tongue

TABLE OF CONTENTS

Introduction 1

#1 Anticipate Impromptu Speaking Situations 9

#2 Know 3 Things: Your Audience, Yourself & Your Stuff 17

#3 Be Present: Pay Attention & Listen Actively 28

#4 Buy Time When Called on Unexpectedly 34

#5 Use Impromptu Speaking Frameworks 45

#6 Tell a Relevant Story 65

#7 Agree & Build on What Others Say 74

#8 Handle Criticism or Conflict In-the-Moment 79

#9 Interrupt When Necessary 86

#10 Convey Confidence with Your Voice & Body Language 93

Conclusion 102

References 104

Appendix A: Impromptu Topics 105

Appendix B: Tips for Specific Impromptu Situations 108

About the Author 119

INTRODUCTION

Has someone ever asked you a question and your mind went blank? Or, maybe you blathered on, hoping you eventually found a point to make, but instead, you repeated yourself and rambled on as the other person's eyes glazed over?

The first time I remember drawing a blank was in my high school English class. The teacher was droning on about some arcane point in Romeo and Juliet and then asked a question. I don't remember the question, only that the teacher ended it with, "What do you think, Diane?"

Hearing my name startled me. I hadn't been paying attention. Immediately, my stomach seemed to flip upside down, and my face became hot. All eyes were on me. Some students looked at me with superiority because they had an answer, but most looked at me with empathy and relief that the teacher didn't call on them.

After a few panicked seconds, I managed a lame, "Could... Could you repeat the question?" which signaled to everyone that I hadn't heard a word before hearing my name. The teacher repeated the question, backing up a little to give me the context. Although I did have an opinion, I was so rattled that I just said, "I really don't know." The teacher pursed his lips and gave me a sidelong glance that clearly communicated that he was disappointed in my answer. I wanted to disappear.

As I became a young adult, I felt it was better to start talking when someone asked me a question rather than let the empty silence hang like a guillotine blade over my head. This approach left the listener wondering what my point was and if I would ever make it. Some people politely waited; others would fidget, their movements giving away their desire to escape my repetitious and rambling answers.

Then, I was employed as an engineer and felt that in replying to a question, I should build up my case and logically support my point before making the point. This approach made sense but I slowly realized how exasperating this approach was when it was used on me. When others used the "build-up to the point" approach, I recall wondering... *So, what's the point?* I wondered if there was an approach to answering questions that didn't involve rambling or the excruciating build-up to a point.

Having children was an "ah-ha" moment for me. Small children have no patience for rambling or long, drawn-out explanations. It was best to get to the point quickly and concisely.

Not: "Having a tidy living area makes it easier to find things and prevents potential tripping injuries. Trips and falls are the leading cause of unintentional home injury and cause 43% of home injury deaths. I'm sure you don't want anyone to get hurt. So, to prevent injuries to your beloved family members and avoid the punishment of grounding, pick up your Legos."

Instead: "Your Legos are a mess and dangerous. Pick up your Legos now, or you're grounded!"

While direct clarity was easy with my children, in many other situations, I was still flustered.

In conversations with people I didn't know well, I hesitated in speaking up. Instead, I coped by encouraging others to talk, so I didn't have to.

In meetings, I was often silent, letting other, louder voices dominate and letting my good ideas swirl in my head, rarely speaking up. Sometimes I would even hear someone else take credit for an idea I had mentioned in a conversation.

And then, I joined Toastmasters*, a worldwide organization to empower people to become more effective communicators and leaders. The Toastmasters program allows people to practice communication and leadership skills in a peer-led environment. One typical feature of most club meetings is an impromptu-speaking segment called Table Topics. A Topic Master typically asks a question and then calls on a member to respond. The goal is to speak coherently on the topic for 1-2 minutes. When it was Table Topics time, I would look down and not make eye contact with the Topic Master, hoping he would call on someone else. Inevitably, I would be called on. The first time, I spoke for a whopping 10 seconds. Over time, I observed how others would answer the question with delay tactics, such as repeating the question or even pivoting to a different topic. I could do that, too! So, if I was asked about something like football, a topic I know little about, I could pivot. I could say something like, "Football is a sport I only know from performing in the marching band at half-time..." and then go into a story about marching band.

Over time, with more life experience, and a few improv classes, I became much better at impromptu speaking and speaking in general.

I took what once scared me and made a business out of it, Virtual Speech Coach, in which I train and coach subject matter experts to speak with confidence and clarity.

During the Covid-19 pandemic, many prospective clients contacted me about improving their impromptu speaking skills for work or their businesses. They wanted to speak off-the-top of their heads without sounding like they had lost their minds. So, I created an impromptu speaking coaching program. In the program, they could learn impromptu speaking strategies and practice several impromptu speaking frameworks to speak clearly, succinctly, and with confidence in real-life situations, such as:

- Job interviews
- Client, Customer & Co-worker interactions

- Conflict situations
- Meetings
- Q&A Sessions
- Short-notice speeches

But, beyond the day-to-day use of impromptu speaking, you may be called to speak from the heart and stir an audience to action, just like Dr. Martin Luther King Jr. did as he spoke in front of the Lincoln Memorial on August 28, 1963, with a carefully planned speech in front of him. And then he went off-script, setting the written speech aside. He said, "…I still have a dream." And he continued, without notes, giving the part of the speech celebrated by history as the "I Have a Dream" speech. He had used the phrase 'I have a dream' many times before, so he was well-acquainted with the words and the concepts, but it wasn't in the prepared text. It was the perfect juxtaposition of when preparedness and opportunity meet.

Will you be prepared to rise to the occasion when given the opportunity?

In this book, you will learn the top strategies that have helped my clients and others speak up and get heard in impromptu speaking opportunities.

The strategies can be summarized in the 5 Ps of impromptu speaking:

Prepare. Presence. Patterns. Partner. Poise.

PREPARE—Prepare by anticipating impromptu speaking situations and knowing yourself, your audience, and your "stuff."

PRESENCE—Be present by paying attention, listening actively, and interrupting if necessary.

PATTERNS—Use patterns for buying time, structuring responses, and including stories.

PARTNER—Create a partnering mindset as you agree and build on what others say or deal with conflict situations.

POISE—Be poised to convey confidence with your voice & body language.

Learn and apply these strategies to help you speak clearly and confidently in impromptu speaking situations, to "Think on Your Feet without Tripping Over Your Tongue!"

Toastmasters International is a world leader in communication and leadership development, with a global network of meeting locations spanning 149 countries worldwide. Through its proven educational program, the 300,000 members of its 15,800 clubs are empowered to develop their speaking and leadership skills, facilitating greater self-confidence and personal growth. To learn more about Toastmasters International, visit www.toastmasters.org.

#1 ANTICIPATE IMPROMPTU SPEAKING SITUATIONS

"Fortune favors the prepared mind." —Louis Pasteur

Students, staff, and parents filled the church auditorium. Five well-dressed high school seniors sat in a neat row at the front, waiting nervously to give their speeches. I had been invited to attend because I had met with them (and all the other seniors) in brief coaching sessions to review their written speeches. The "Final 5" speakers had been selected as presenting the best of the personal testimonial-type speeches at their Christian school.

When their well-delivered speeches were done and the judges had turned in their ballots, I pulled out my phone and scrolled through emails. Then I heard the head of the school introduce me. He asked me to "come up and say a few words" about the students' speeches.

"What? What am I going to say?"

I momentarily panicked. I had not anticipated speaking. But it would look bad for the speech coach to be at a loss for words.

Fortunately, I had taken brief notes during their speeches. I had jotted down each student's name, the speech title, and a couple of things that left an impact. As I walked up to the lectern, I clutched the notes like a drowning man clutches a life preserver.

As I smiled at the "final 5" and then at the rest of the audience (buying a few seconds), a relevant quote from Proverbs came to mind. I began, "In the Bible, it says, 'A word fitly spoken is like apples of gold.' Today's speeches certainly left us with some golden ideas to ponder..." and then I simply pointed out the best parts of each speech and finished with thanking the students.

Whew! Impromptu speaking crisis averted.

I was fortunate to have taken a few notes and that an opening had come to mind. But, in hindsight, I realized I should have had the foresight to anticipate that I might have to speak.

Unless you are called in at the last moment to attend an event, you have some time to prepare. Always assume that you will be called upon. You can prepare, generally, for almost any occasion and specifically, for events such as the ones in the list below (See Appendix II for tips in handling these specific situations)

- Meetings
- Job Interviews
- Media interviews
- Weddings and other celebrations
- Social events
- Networking events

General preparation includes building anticipatory skills, learning impromptu speaking approaches and frameworks, and practicing impromptu speaking.

There are several ways to practice impromptu speaking. You can practice dinnertime topics with your family or friends, with topics written on slips of paper in a "topic jar" or with one main discussion topic to which everyone contributes. You can even practice on your own by choosing a random topic to speak about. **See Appendix 1** for some impromptu speaking topics. You also could join a Toastmasters club. Most clubs have an impromptu speaking portion of the meeting called Table Topics, during which members are called on to respond to a speaking prompt.

Anticipatory skills are techniques used to decrease response time to a stimulus. Building anticipatory skills can make it seem like you can predict the future or are prepared for almost anything. These techniques are most clearly observed in athletics. Unless you have participated in a sport, you may not wholly appreciate the skill.

Maybe you have experienced this: you watch a sport, think, "That looks fun," try it, and then discover it is far more challenging than you initially thought. I know I felt that way about Taekwondo (a Korean form of martial arts). I had watched my children's Taekwondo classes and gave it a try.

Eventually, I purchased sparring gear, protective head, hand, and foot coverings, shin guards, and a mouthguard. I suited up for my first match, feeling anxious but well-protected. My sparring partner was a 12-year-old girl. *How hard could it be?*

Really hard, as it turned out.

We squared off, bowed to each other, and got in fighting stances. The head instructor yelled, "Fight!"

I got ready to punch and pow! She swiftly punched my gut and managed a kick to my head even though she was several inches shorter. I hadn't seen it coming. The rest of our 2-minute match continued similarly. I felt like a blind sloth trying to swat at an ever-moving fly.

I sat out the next round and stood against the wall next to a more experienced fighter. "Watch her feet," he said, referring to my previous sparring partner. "See how she telegraphs her kick by raising on her toes early with her other leg. She dips her shoulder, too."

I did see it! It was a revelation that I could anticipate an opponent's moves by noticing visual clues in their preparatory body language. I had a new appreciation for athletic competitions. Although I never developed the attack speed of many of my opponents, at least I could anticipate the punches and kicks better and block more of them.

Anticipation is vital in sports and impromptu speaking situations. You can predict what is likely to happen, foresee the actions of others, and sometimes even proactively act to create a more favorable outcome.

You can build your anticipatory skills in several ways, including:

1. **Horizon gazing.** Look out across the landscape of time, beyond the moment, toward the rest of the day, the rest of the week, or even longer. Pull out your calendar and note upcoming meetings and other planned or likely interactions. Ask yourself, *what might I be asked? What might I be expected to contribute? Should I talk to some people ahead of time? What can I prepare ahead of time?*

2. **Mental simulation.** Create a mental model of the situation and run a few simulations of different if-then scenarios. *"If this happens, then I will say/do that..."*

3. **Clues.** Pay attention to communication, or lack of communication, body language, facial expressions, and vocal inflection before and during social interactions—more on this in Chapter 3.

Using the techniques of horizon gazing, mental simulation, and clues in an example:

Let's say you are looking at upcoming meetings in your calendar (horizon gazing) and notice a project status meeting at 1 PM tomorrow. You review the meeting attendees and notice that your boss will be attending (clues). You ask yourself, *what might I be asked? What might I be expected to contribute? Should I talk to some people ahead of time?* And, since your boss will be there, *what does my boss expect?*

You mentally answer (maybe even jotting down notes). *I might be asked about progress, obstacles, and customer input. I might be expected to contribute both data and recommendations. My boss wants me to speak up more in meetings. He probably wants me to make him look good. Maybe I should touch base with him today and see what his expectations are of me at the meeting.*

You might try a few if/then scenarios (mental simulation). *If I am asked about progress, then I will get to the point and say we are a week behind schedule due to some team members being out but anticipate catching up by the end of the month, with people working a little overtime.*

If I'm asked about obstacles, then I will let them know there is a supply issue with a critical part, but we can look at other vendors.

If I'm asked about customer input, then I can share the results of a recent customer survey and make recommendations for minor modifications to improve the user experience.

Now, even if you aren't asked about specific questions or scenarios you imagined, you may still have the opportunity to bring up the issues and meet your boss's expectation of speaking up more in meetings.

Build your anticipatory skills and build your confidence in speaking up.

#2 KNOW 3 THINGS: YOUR AUDIENCE, YOURSELF & YOUR STUFF

"Knowledge is power." —Francis Bacon

Knowledge is power. Or at least the potential for power.

With knowledge of your audience, yourself, and your "stuff" (content), you have the potential to significantly increase your ability to have something valuable to say when you speak up.

Know Your Audience

The more you know your audience, the more you are likely to connect when you speak off-the-cuff. You can know general demographic information (e.g., age, gender, education level, location, culture, income, race, occupation, marital status, affiliations). You can know psychographic traits (e.g., personality, values, attitudes, interests, beliefs). You may even know more specific, unique issues that concern them (e.g., pain points and preferred communication styles).

Not knowing your audience can cause awkward situations, especially in cross-cultural communication.

A few years ago, I was a virtual speaker for a conference in Iran. As the meeting planner and I exchanged text messages, I sent a thumbs-up emoji to indicate agreement. There was a long pause before I got a reply. As I waited for a reply, I realized maybe I had made a cultural misstep with that thumbs-up emoji, so I googled, "Thumbs up Iran." The first Google result revealed my error. A thumbs up in Iran is an indecent and offensive insult. Yikes. I quickly texted an apology for my innocent mistake. Fortunately, the meeting planner understood what I meant and found the situation amusing.

Not knowing your audience can be a career-killer.

You are likely to communicate with people with different job responsibilities. They have different concerns and different levels of knowledge and experience. If you don't tailor your communication to your specific work audience, you risk being annoying and irrelevant.

Imagine this common scenario. You are in a meeting with upper management, and they ask you a question about the project you are leading, such as, "Will we be able to meet the deadlines with the existing staff?" This is your chance to shine! You know every detail of the project and dive right into the deep end of your planning process and staff allocations, building the case for hiring a couple of extra people, but 5 minutes in, you still haven't answered the question. You don't even notice the heavy sighs and sideways glances. You can't hear the voices in their heads, but they are silently pleading, "Please, just get to the point!"

How you structure a response can make a huge difference in how it is received. You will learn more about impromptu speaking frameworks in chapter 5. In this chapter, the focus is on choosing the content in your communication. Tailoring your communication style and content will enhance the reception of your message.

Now, you may not have a lot of time to analyze your audience and adjust your communication in some impromptu situations. Still, three fundamental questions can help you tailor your content when asked to contribute to a meeting or respond to a question:

1. Why do they care?
2. What do they know?
3. Why did they ask me?

"Why do they care?"

Asking this question will guide your response based on their motivation to hear what you have to say. Do they need to make a decision? Should they pass on the information to someone else? Are they concerned about something? Think about why they would care given their job responsibilities.

"What do they know?"

Asking this question will guide your response based on their knowledge of the material or the situation, so you don't talk above or below their level of understanding.

"Why did they ask me?"

Asking this question will guide your response based on what value you bring. Why are they asking you and not someone else? Why were you invited to the meeting or conversation? How can your answer help them in their goals or business objectives?

A mental shortcut to knowing your audience is to take their perspective on a situation, taking on their viewpoint.

At work, different perspectives can arise on a topic when people have specialized knowledge of a topic or are focused only on one aspect of a topic. Let's say two engineers are talking about "product design." One engineer, fresh out of college, believes that you must always design the most elegant product, innovative and easy to use, no matter the cost. The other engineer, with 20 years of experience, believes that you need to optimize the design within the constraints of time and money set by management. The more experienced engineer, without thinking, might grimace and make disparaging remarks about idealism vs. reality. That approach could be a conversation-killer. Instead, the more experienced engineer could look at the situation from the viewpoint of the idealistic and inexperienced younger engineer and invite discussion by finding an area of agreement, "The best design is ideal..."

Before you can easily take others' perspectives, you must know yourself and the basis for your perspective in different situations.

Know Yourself

Knowing others is important in communication but knowing yourself is crucial. Aristotle said, "Knowing yourself is the beginning of all wisdom." A little self-reflection, especially knowing your values, can go a long way in helping you communicate clearly and authentically, even in impromptu situations. Your values are your moral compass, guiding how you behave and what you say. You can speak more decisively if you know your values, framing your words within your values.

For example, two of my top values are honesty and kindness. A client asked me my opinion on an email she sent her boss. The email rambled, had a couple of minor grammatical mistakes, and contained a sentence in all capital letters. I'm thinking, "*Too bad she didn't ask my opinion before she sent it.*" But it would have been unkind for me to say that or to nit-pick every issue with the email. So, I asked her, "What are you concerned about?" hoping that she didn't want a blow-by-blow (plus, asking questions is a delay technique, you will learn more about in Chapter 4). But she just wanted me to comment on the "tone." I honestly, and with kindness, first pointed out what she did well regarding tone, such as being polite and positive. After that, I pointed out the most egregious tone violation, the all-caps sentence (and offered suggestions for alternative ways to emphasize important information).

To clarify your values, ask yourself what is important to you and why. If you say, "My family is important to me," why is your family important? Is it because you value connection, loyalty, leaving a legacy, or something else? What is meaningful to you? What inspires you to persevere? It's helpful to pick 5-7 of your top values from one of the many lists you can find online.

Knowing yourself also means understanding that you have a perspective on a topic. Your perspective is based on your experiences, which may differ so much from others' that your communication may not have the desired effect. For example, when my daughter was about 3, I showed her how to use a computer for the first time. I placed a few books on the chair in front of my computer desk so she could comfortably see the screen and move the mouse. She wanted to move an object on the screen, so I placed her hand on the mouse and told her to move it up. She promptly lifted the mouse vertically off the surface of the table. Her interpretation of my words momentarily blew my mind. I realized that I had instructed her based on my perspective on moving a computer mouse.

Knowing yourself and your audience will help you frame your communication authentically and in a way that your audience can understand. But you also must know what you are talking about.

Know Your Stuff

One challenge in many impromptu speaking situations is that you are put on the spot to say something relevant about a topic. Building your future-predicting anticipatory skills (Chapter 1) and using impromptu speaking frameworks (Chapter 5) can set the stage for sounding confident. However, you still need content and some substance to what you say.

Depending on your area of expertise, you can learn in several ways—from formal education to self-education to on-the-job experience. Gaining job experience takes time, but you can seek short classes, books, and other information sources if you need to learn specific information quickly. But then you need a plan to learn the material. Some techniques to increase your memory and recall include:

1. **Visualize.** Visualize the information as pictures. What you see, you remember.
2. **Associate.** Associate the information with something you already know.
3. **Chunk.** Break up the information into smaller, easier-to-digest pieces.
4. **Repeat.** Use spaced repetition. Study or practice at regular intervals.
5. **Write.** Write it out in your own words, by hand.
6. **Test.** Test yourself.
7. **Teach.** Teach someone else (or discuss).

Years ago, I was a cognitive skills trainer for a business focusing on one-on-one cognitive skills training (i.e., "brain training"). One of the brain training activities was memorizing the presidents of the United States in order. I had never done this myself, so I had to apply the training techniques to myself.

The company provided a training aid that enabled the visualization and association of the presidents' names. First, each name had an associated picture. For example, "Madison" was a mad sun, "Adams" was an atom, and "Monroe" was a man rowing. Then each picture was associated or linked with the next. The mad sun (Madison) had a man rowing (Monroe) on one of its sunbeams. The oar on the rowboat was super-powered by an atom (Adams). Madison-Monroe-Adams. I had to learn to tell the entire list of presidents in order by visualizing and associating name pictures. I chunked this task into smaller parts, of about ten presidents per day, spending just a few minutes each day reviewing the previous associations and adding on about ten new presidents. To reinforce the associations, I also practiced them backward. I tested myself each day, timing my recitation and then doing it a few more times, trying to beat my time. At the end of the week, I had my first student and helped him learn to recite the names of all the presidents in order. Teaching others reinforced my own learning.

Knowing your stuff, yourself, and your audience won't do much good if you don't know how to pay attention!

#3 BE PRESENT: PAY ATTENTION & LISTEN ACTIVELY

"Multitasking divides your attention and leads to confusion and weakened focus." —Deepak Chopra

Hello?

Are you here?

Really here?

Not multi-tasking?

Not thinking about something else, but fully present?

Or are you distracted?

Distractions can be deadly (e.g., texting while driving). Distractions can affect your productivity. Distractions can even reduce your ability to respond in impromptu speaking situations.

Which of the following have been distractions for you?

- Phone/texting
- Email

- Chat messages
- Social media/notifications
- Food
- Coworkers
- Extraneous noise
- Pets
- Family
- Personal problems
- Multi-tasking
- Fatigue
- Illness
- Other?

Which distractions can you eliminate or reduce? Go through the list and pick your top distractions. Then, take action to mitigate the distraction. Remove the cues that trigger distraction wherever possible. For example, if your phone is a distraction, consider turning off notifications or turning it face down. If family or coworkers interrupt you, put a "Do Not Disturb" sign where they can't miss it.

The biggest distraction for me and many people, especially when in online meetings, is multi-tasking.

It's easy to be lured by the siren song of multitasking efficiency.

In Greek mythology, the sirens were creatures with enchanting voices who lured sailors to their deaths on rocky coasts. The Greek hero Odysseus was curious about their songs but knew he had to prevent his crew from hearing the sirens. He cleverly eliminated the deadly distraction by having his crew physically restrain him, tying him to the mast while plugging their own ears with beeswax. You might not use beeswax, but if you don't take proactive steps, you can be drawn into destruction by believing you can be more productive when multi-tasking.

Multitasking is a myth.

Much research has exposed the myth of multi-tasking, pointing out that our brains don't do tasks simultaneously. Instead, we just switch tasks quickly with a stop/start process. This task-switching takes time and energy and reduces our focus.

It is so tempting to multi-task, especially in online meetings. I admit to trying to be stealthy about reading emails and doing other tasks, putting my browser and mail applications in dark mode, trying to avoid the telltale flash of light when the screen brightens. But occasionally, someone asking for my input would surprise me, and I would have to admit I wasn't paying attention or ask them to repeat the question.

Resist the urge to multi-task. Even better, eliminate the cues that trigger multitasking behavior. For example, when in an online meeting, close your email application or anything else that might vie for your attention.

The second biggest distraction for most people in impromptu speaking situations is their own thoughts about the situation. All too often, people aren't listening to understand but just waiting to respond. They are thinking about their responses and not paying close attention to what others communicate. This can lead them to respond so it makes others feel they haven't been heard.

So, assuming you have reduced distractions, how else can you pay attention in conversations or meetings, focus on what is being said, and be ready to answer questions or provide input as an active listener?

For many, the easiest method to focus attention is to take notes on paper. Pull out a notebook or a piece of paper and a pen and write down important points in the meeting or conversation—ideas, decisions, and action items. Plus, if you have an extraneous thought, such as, "I need to get kitty litter at the store," or, "I need to remind Chris about the client call," write those down so you can clear your mind for the discussion at hand. If part of the meeting doesn't seem relevant, you can discretely doodle to give yourself something to do.

Besides helping you focus, jotting down notes gives you some ready-made content when asked to respond. You can "take a step back" and summarize what has been said, offering a recap, before adding your input, or you can mention something someone else said as a segue to your point. In conversations, when you repeat or paraphrase what the other person has said, you also make them feel heard, like you were listening and understood them. Or, if you aren't clear on what they said, you can ask them to clarify your understanding, with leading phrases, such as, "It sounds like you're saying...," or, "Am I correct in understanding... ?"

As you take notes (or even if you don't), pay attention to more than just the spoken words. Watch for non-verbal communication clues (body language, facial expressions, tone of voice, and expressions of emotion). Someone may say, "That's brilliant," but their non-verbal communication can change the meaning.

"That's brilliant!" said with a smile and excitement is a positive statement.

"That's brilliant," said with an eye-roll and an up and down sarcastic tone is a negative statement, meaning the exact opposite of the words.

How you respond depends on how well you pay attention to the entire communication.

The not-so-simple act of paying attention can take you a long way.

#4 BUY TIME WHEN CALLED ON UNEXPECTEDLY

"Silence is golden when you can't think of a good answer." —Muhammad Ali

There are many impromptu situations and questions you can anticipate, but often they come out of left field, surprising you when you least expect them.

Maybe you're interviewing for a job, and the interviewer asks you an odd question, such as, "If you could be any animal for a day, which would you be and why?" (I'd be very tempted to turn that question back to the interviewer, "What an intriguing question! Which animal would you be?" Ah, I've already revealed a delay tactic!).

Or maybe you're attending a work meeting just to be informed about a project you aren't directly involved in, and someone asks you for your opinion. A momentary panic grips your gut, your heart races, and your mind gropes for a relevant response. You blurt out something that leaves people furrowing their brows in confusion. And then, your brain regains control, and you mage to add some useful information. At least there was that. But what if you'd had just a bit more time before you spoke?

Sometimes, you need just a little more time; time to grasp a concept, formulate your thoughts, clarify the question, and time to breathe.

A few common delay tactics (some of which can be combined):

- Pause for a breath
- Repeat or rephrase the question
- Clarify the question
- Talk about the question
- Answer part of the question
- Acknowledge and pivot
- Repeat your own or someone else's words
- Take a step back & summarize
- Ask for time to think about it/get more information
- Defer the highly technical question
- Take a sip of water

- Turn it over to someone else

Pause for a breath

A pause of 3-5 seconds has many advantages: it increases your mental clarity, gives you time to think, and makes you look deliberate and more confident.

When you are asked an unanticipated question, your brain may interpret it as a threat, and you may experience fight or flight response symptoms, including increased heart rate, breathing rate, and blood pressure. You are going into survival mode, and your higher-level thinking may be compromised. Taking a deep breath or two can reduce anxiety and help you think more clearly.

A pause also gives you time to formulate a response, which may start with rephrasing or clarifying the question, which buys you even more time.

A pause can give the impression of thoughtful deliberation and confidence. When you pause, it is an indication you are listening to what is being said and are processing a response. Blurting out an answer can signal nervousness or indicate that you weren't really listening but only waiting for your turn to speak.

To practice pausing, even when you can answer right away, try taking an extra breath before answering.

Repeat or rephrase the question

Repeating or rephrasing a question not only buys time but it ensures that you and the questioner understand the question. Yes, you read that correctly. Sometimes the person asking the question doesn't fully understand what they are asking. Repeating the question and showing you understand the question (or not) also lets the questioner hear their question, which may encourage them to modify or clarify their question. Plus, it reduces the likelihood you will spend time answering a question, only to have the questioner say, "No. I wasn't asking that..."

Fortunately, most questions are straightforward. You can listen for keywords to repeat.

Let's say you are at a job interview, and the interviewer asks, "Why do you want to work for our company?"

You can respond, "So, you'd like to know why I want to work here? Okay, ..."

One caveat on repeating the question--If the question is framed with negative words, you might not want to repeat the negative words. For example, let's say you are a coach, and a prospective client asks, "Why are you charging so much for your program?" Rather than repeat, "You are wondering why I charge so much?" You can rephrase the question more positively, such as, "You are wondering whether you are getting a good value for the price, right?" And, then you can speak to a more positive version of the question.

Clarify the question

Some questions are confusing or tricky, such as, "What are five things you could do with a paper clip, other than holding papers together?"

You might respond by repeating/rephrasing the question and then clarifying the intent, indicating what you believe to be the purpose of the question, saying something like, "What are five things that I could do with a paper clip? So, you want some out-of-the-box ideas, right?"

You can lead into clarifying the question with typical lead-in phrases, such as:

"So..."

"So, what you're asking is..."

"What I hear you saying is..."

"Are you saying...?"

"It sounds like..."

"In other words,..."

"From what I understand, you want to know..."

"If I understood you correctly..."

"Correct me if I'm wrong. What you're saying is..."

Talk about the question

You can make a positive statement about a question (never say, "That's a stupid question!"), or break the question into parts.

"That's a great (or fantastic, insightful, or intriguing) question! I'm sure a lot of people here are wondering the same thing..."

"Let's unpack that question… " (useful for a question that is complex).

Narrow the question

You can answer some tough questions in part. You might select to answer a less divisive aspect of a question or just an aspect you can address right away.

"There is one aspect of that question I can answer right now…"

"For now, let's address…" You can offer to discuss other aspects later.

Acknowledge and pivot

Have you ever noticed that politicians often answer a question without answering it? While you might not want to use the common political technique of attacking the question, or the questioner, you can take a page from the politicians' interview playbook: acknowledge the question and divert your answer to another topic or one of your key messages. You may want to redirect a question for many reasons, including pivoting a discussion to a more critical issue or one you feel less vulnerable in answering.

First, acknowledge the question and then pivot.

"That's an interesting question, but a more important concern (or "What I think you really want to know") is..."

"Thank you for that question, but I'd like to point out that..."

Repeat someone else's words

If you have been taking notes, start your answer by repeating what someone else has said related to the question. You not only look like a sharp listener, but you also shine the spotlight on someone else.

"As Ravi said earlier..."

Review: Take a step back & summarize

You can summarize the discussion before answering the question.

"Let me take a step back, to make sure I understand everything first..."

Or you can frame it as a benefit to all.

"Let's take a step back to make sure we are all on the same page. We've covered a lot so far..."

Ask for time to think about it/get more information

Another technique is to say you don't have enough information to provide an adequate answer at the moment to a question. Buy yourself some time by saying, "I'll need to get back to you on that so I can give you a full answer (or better, or complete answer). I can get back to you in (time frame).

You can also give a reason why you can't answer right away.

"I need to do some research (or dig a little deeper) before I can answer that."

"I don't want to give you the wrong information, so let me check with [name/department] and get back to you."

Defer the highly technical question

Sometimes you may be asked a highly technical or rather esoteric question that only the questioner (or a tiny portion of the audience) would be interested in. In this case, you can defer the question to a later time by saying something such as, "That's an interesting question and one that probably only you and I really want to dig into. Let me discuss that with you after the meeting."

Take a sip of water

It's a good idea to have something to sip on during a meeting. Not only can you quench your thirst, but you can also delay answering or extend a pause a bit longer by taking a sip of water or other beverage. Sip slowly, calmly, and have a thoughtful look on your face, even if your mind is in overdrive trying to compose your thoughts.

Turn it over to someone else

Sometimes you aren't the best person to answer a question, or you want to shine the light on another team member, empowering them by asking them to provide input. Ideally, you will make a few comments or provide your insight before turning it over to someone else.

"You know, our project leader, Sue, has been working on that very issue. Sue, what are your thoughts?"

Occasionally, you can even turn the question back on the questioner.

"That's a great question! What are your thoughts on the matter?"

Putting it into Practice

To get started with delay tactics, focus on the first two: Pause & Repeat. Pause a few seconds and then repeat (or rephrase the question) as you formulate an answer. You can also pay attention to how other people respond to questions. What techniques do they use?

#5 USE IMPROMPTU SPEAKING FRAMEWORKS

"Be not careless in deeds, nor confused in words, nor rambling in thought." —Marcus Aurelius

Responding clearly and confidently when called on unexpectedly is easier if you have a pre-planned framework. The number one consideration is to be clear in your mind on your point. If you aren't clear on your point, your listeners won't be either. Sometimes your mind is swirling with several possible points, making it hard to respond. You can deal with this problem by acknowledging there are several possibilities and then just pick one, to begin with.

For example, let's say someone asks me, "What is your favorite food?" I consider this question and think, *I like so many different foods, I can't pick a favorite!* I could use some delay tactics such as pausing, repeating the question, or pivoting the question to my least favorite food. Or I could just pick one of my favorite foods and say something like, "There are many foods I like to eat. One of my favorite foods is Brussels sprouts. I know you probably didn't expect Brussels sprouts as a favorite food, but let me tell you why I love Brussels sprouts..."

There are many possible approaches you can use. Some approaches are straightforward and logical, such as explaining the sequence of steps in a process. Other common strategies, frameworks for which I will provide additional details, are:

- P.R.E.P. (Point, Reason, Example, Point)—Get to the point
- The 30-second Meeting Update
- What/Why/How—Get buy-in
- 5 Ws (Who, What, When, Where, Why)—Give specific direction for action
- Problem/Cause/Solution—Build to a logical solution
- Issue/Pros/Cons/Recommendation—Make the well-considered case
- Past/Present/Future— Take them on a journey or cast a vision

- 3 (or more) Perspectives—Look at an issue from different perspectives
- S.T.A.R. (Situation, Task, Action, Result)—Answer behavioral interview questions
- Point/Story/Lesson—Teach a lesson

BEFORE you answer questions, understand why the person is asking you the question (do they need to make a decision or take any action?) and their level of knowledge (so you don't confuse them). You can always ask clarifying questions, such as, "Do you mean…?" It may help to repeat or paraphrase the question.

As you read the description of each framework, pick one to use today that is immediately applicable to your life or in your next meeting or conversation.

P.R.E.P. (Point, Reason, Example, Point)
—Get to the point

The P.R.E.P. framework, from the book, Speaking Up: Surviving Executive Presentations, is my go-to framework, the one I use most often to answer questions clearly, getting to the point right away.

Getting to the point right away is essential, especially when talking with executives or with busy people who may not have a deep understanding of your topic. By getting to the point first, you give context for your supporting comments (reason and example). If you try to answer questions by building up to your point (for example, by sharing a test result before stating a point), you are likely to confuse and annoy the person who asked you the question).

P.R.E.P. is an acronym:

Point –state your point or position

Reason (why/because) –state a reason you have for your point or position

Example (evidence/story) –usually an example

Point (restate)—restate your point or position

Let's say you ask me, "What is your favorite food?"

I might respond,

Point: "There are many foods I like to eat. One of my favorite foods is Brussels sprouts.

Reason: "I know you probably didn't expect Brussels sprouts as a favorite food but let me tell you why I love

Brussels sprouts. They are healthy, and they taste great, especially when roasted."

(Note: I gave two reasons. I could talk about each cause, or just pick one.)

Example: "Growing up, I hated Brussels sprouts. They were so stinky and bitter. It wasn't until I was an adult that I realized there was a cooking method that made them taste good. I watched a cooking show, and the chef roasted the Brussels sprouts in the oven with a little olive oil and seasoning. The guests on the show sang the praises of the caramelized Brussels sprouts. So, I gave it a try. I couldn't believe how delicious they were. And, so healthy, too, with fiber and other nutrients. I'd rather eat roasted Brussels sprouts than chocolate."

Point (restatement): "That's how Brussels sprouts went from a food I hated to one of my favorite foods."

Variation 1: P.R.P. (Point, Reason, Point): Not every answer needs an example (evidence/story), but many points can be better understood and remembered with additional support. Also, if you ramble or meander in your response, you can still sound more organized by restating your point at the end.

Variation 2: P.E.P. (Point, Example, Point): Sometimes, you can make a point, offer a story that illustrates the point, and then wrap up by restating your main point.

The 30-second Meeting Update

For an update at a meeting, you generally want to be brief. You can give a meeting update, with four basic steps in about 30 seconds:

Step 1: Introduction/Bottom line status: In one sentence, state the bottom-line status

Step 2: Give 2-3 relevant points (1-3 sentences)

Step 3: Conclusion: give a one-sentence conclusion

Step 4: Call-to-Action (optional): Ask for action or let them know how to contact you to follow up.

For example, if you are giving an update on vendor selection, the update might be something like this:

Introduction (Bottom line status): "We've narrowed the potential software vendors to the top 3 choices."

2-3 Relevant Points: "We originally received eight vendor bids. After reviewing their proposals, we shortlisted the top three to demo to the procurement team next week. And in a couple of weeks, we'll schedule one or more in-depth demos with key stakeholders."

Conclusion: "We expect to select a vendor by the end of the month."

Call-to-Action (optional): "Let me know by Friday if you want to be invited to next week's short demos."

What/Why/How

The What/Why/How format is a straightforward, easy-to-remember way to communicate a concept quickly, clearly, and persuasively.

Briefly address what you are talking about. You may need to provide some context. Then move quickly to why it is important or why the audience would care. Finally, give them the next step, or tell them how to take action.

For example, if you are talking about an upcoming event, and someone asks what needs to happen to make it profitable, you might answer, especially if you are in the PR department, something like: "From a PR perspective, we need to promote the event to our target audience *(what)*. Any event needs people to attend to make it successful. No people. No ticket sales. No sponsors. No money *(why)*. Our first step needs to be a promotional plan *(how)*."

5 Ws—Speak like a journalist about an event

The 5Ws framework is particularly useful when you talk about a specific event. You can approach the topic like a journalist and address the who, what, when, where, and why. You can even follow the order, starting with the who, to identify the main characters, and ending with the why, to end on the most compelling point.

1. Who: Who is organizing, working, or attending the event?
2. What: What is the event? What are the goals? What are the tasks?
3. When: When is the event? What is the project timeline?
4. Where: Where will the event be held?
5. **Why: Why is the event important? To the organization? To the participants?**

For example, if you are talking about a non-profit fundraising event, you could address who founded the non-profit, who will work it, who will attend it, what the theme and goals of the event are, when the event is, where it will be held, and why it is important.

Problem/Cause/Solution—Build to a logical solution

To address an issue using the logical Problem/Cause/Solution framework, you need to clearly understand and explain the problem, as well as the underlying causes and the proposed solution. The trickiest part of this approach is understanding the root causes of a problem; otherwise, you may suggest an ineffective solution.

You can qualify your perspective on a problem:

"The problem, as I see it is... " (clearly explain the problem from your perspective, in terms your audience can understand)

"The root cause of the problem is... " (explain what has caused the problem)

"The best/most cost-effective solution would be..." (what makes the proposed solution the best choice)

Issue/Pros/Cons/Recommendation—Make the well-considered case

You may be asked to make a recommendation based on your expertise, experience, or evidence (research, input from others).

A common way to present a recommendation is to state the issue and then examine the pros (advantages) and the cons (disadvantages) before giving a recommendation. By providing both pros and cons, you come across as having balanced thinking. Depending on your recommendation, you can choose to present the cons before the pros. You probably want to end with the pros if you are for something. If you are against something, you probably want to end with the cons.

Let's say you are discussing with your family whether you should get a cat (and you want to get a cat, so you will end on the pros). You might say something like:

Issue: "Should we get a cat? Let's look at some of the pros and cons."

Cons: Some reasons not to get a cat could include:

- Some cats are aloof
- You must clean the litter box
- They don't provide protection from intruders

Pros: But there are good reasons to have a cat as a pet:

- They are independent
- They can be entirely indoors
- They are relatively quiet

Recommendation: "For our busy lifestyle, I think a cat would be a good choice as a pet."

That example was bare bones. You can add more detail to each of your reasons if you want.

Past/Present/Future—Take them on a journey or cast a vision

The "past, present, future" model for structuring communications is helpful in answering questions and casting a vision for the future.

When answering a question about future actions/decisions, you can use these steps:

1. Repeat the question
2. Past: Tell what was done in the past
3. Present: Tell what is being done now in the present
4. Future: Tell what you think should be done in the future
5. Make a summary statement

For example, let's say someone asks me, "Is breakfast an important meal?"

Using the five steps above, I might answer like this:

1. Repeat the question: "Is breakfast an important meal?" (pause)
2. Past: "For many years, I believed breakfast to be the most important meal of the day and would make a big breakfast first thing in the morning."
3. Present: "Recently, my thinking on that has changed, and I now believe that delaying the first meal, creating a longer fasting time, is healthier for many adults."

4. Future: "I will be working on delaying my first meal until lunch and not eating after 8 PM, creating a 16-hour fasting window most days."
5. Summary: "So, I believe breakfast, the first meal of the day, is still important, but that 'breaking the fast' should be done later in the day."

When casting a vision for the future for your project, product, service, team, or organization, the past, present, future format is both clear and compelling.

You can structure an impromptu presentation that makes you sound like a clear visionary by using a "past, present, future" speech format. You can take your listeners on a path from the past to the future! Casting a vision this way shows how we learn from the past, correctly assess the present, and look to a different and better future.

Each element connects with people emotionally:

- Discussing the past builds an emotional connection if you discuss shared history.
- Discussing the present builds connection through continued shared history and strikes

an emotional chord if you speak to a fear of loss if there isn't change.
- Discussing the vision of the future builds connection when there is a call to action to achieve it as a group.

You can even use the same 5-part format to answer an impromptu question.

1. Opening statement on the issue and its importance
2. Past: Share the relevant history
3. Present: What is happening now, and why there needs to be change
4. Future: What is the vision
5. Summary statement/call-to-action

2 (or more) Perspectives—Look at an issue from different perspectives

Multiple perspectives improve the understanding of any situation. When you want to build understanding beyond one perspective (or even just stall), you can look at a topic from different lenses of perspective.

Some examples:

Different Departments: Sales, Manufacturing, Engineering

Different Sensory Experiences: Sight, Sound, Touch

Different Demographics: Age, Gender, Race

Different Categories/Aspects: Strengths, Weaknesses, Opportunities, Threats (SWOT)

Different Levels: Corporate, Employee, Customer

For example, let's say someone asks you why the corporate vision statement is important. You could say something like, "The corporate vision statement is important to the organization, the employees, and the customers. The vision statement is important to the organization because... The vision statement is important to the employees because... The vision statement is important to the customer because..."

S.T.A.R. (Situation, Task, Action, Result)—Answer behavioral interview questions

Don't you love it when you are in a job interview and are asked to respond to a prompt such as, "Can you give me an example of how you handle tasks when your project is on a tight deadline?"

These types of questions are called behavioral interview questions, meant to assess your skill level, how you react to stress, and your professionalism. They are questions about how you acted in a specific situation.

A common approach is to use the S.T.A.R. framework to respond to behavioral interview questions. S.T.A.R. is an acronym:

Situation: Start with a bit of context (who, what, when, where, how)

Task: Describe what you were responsible for. Keep it specific but concise

Action: Describe what you did, focusing on desirable traits (initiative, teamwork, leadership, etc.)

Result: Share the outcome and how you contributed to the outcome. If the outcome wasn't that great, what did you learn?

For example, if you are asked, "Can you give me an example of how you handle tasks when your project is on a tight deadline?" You might respond something like this:

Situation: "Every project is slightly different, but most are on a tight deadline. At my current job, part of my responsibilities was to create testing protocols. I was on a team of 3 people, and we were tasked with creating nine protocols in two weeks. It was an ambitious schedule. And then, a few days in, one of the team members became ill. She was going to be out of commission for at least a week.

Task: My manager then split the extra work between the two of us left on the team. My work on the project increased by almost 50%. And it still needed to be done by the original deadline. It was too late to get another person up-to-speed, so the task fell to my remaining team member and me.

Action: After discussing the situation with my teammate, I asked our manager if we could have a reduction of time, temporarily, in our other tasks, to focus on finishing this project on time. She agreed, and we doubled our efforts to complete the protocols.

Result: Thanks to my teammate and to my being proactive in time management, we finished the protocols two days early, just in time to review them with our co-worker who came back from sick leave. We submitted them a day before the deadline. My manager noted the extra effort, and a few months later, I got promoted.

The S.T.A.R. framework has additional applications. You can use it in performance reviews to provide examples of how you exhibit desired traits. You can also use it to present a case study or to explain "what happened" in a situation.

Point/Story/Lesson—Teach a lesson

Next to the P.R.E.P. format, this is one of my favorite impromptu formats, especially for persuading people to change how they think. Stories are concrete, memorable, and connect with emotions. Developing a story for use in impromptu situations will be discussed in more detail in the next chapter.

The framework is three-fold:

- State your point (but not the lesson)
- Illustrate with a story in which you learned something
- Point out the lesson (the take-away)

Here's a personal example I might use in answering a question such as, "What is an important leadership lesson you've learned?"

(Point) "An important leadership lesson I learned was to empower your leaders."

(Story) "Years ago, I led an organization and had a meeting with the ten divisional leaders. Near the start of the meeting, we discussed a book about empowering leaders, which we had read as a group. Then we continued with the agenda. At the end of the meeting, I asked if there were any concerns, and one of the divisional leaders said, 'Yes. You disempowered us when you had your assistant contact our groups to see if tasks were being completed. You should have talked with us first.' Most of the other division leaders nodded their heads in agreement. Ouch! I had sent out an email about it, but, clearly, an email about what I planned on doing was not the right approach. I hadn't given them a choice, and only a few had even read the email (I hadn't even asked for confirmation). I took a breath, apologized, and we discussed how to handle efforts in a more empowering way. They wanted me to get their buy-in before acting within their divisions."

(Lesson) "I learned an important lesson that day about empowering your leaders: If you want to empower your leaders, don't help them without their buy-in."

#6 TELL A RELEVANT STORY

"If you have a point, find a story." —Og Mandino

Often when called upon to respond to a question, provide input, or "to say a few words," the easiest and most memorable way to respond is to make your point by telling a relevant story.

Six Tips for Impromptu Storytelling:

1. The story must relate to your point. No meandering stories that leave your listener wondering what your point is. Ideally, you will state your point before telling your story and then wrap it up by restating it after your story (or having a call-to-action or a lesson learned).

2. Ideally, use your own stories. You can run the story in your mind like a movie and tell what happened. It's easier to speak without preparation when the events happen to you.

3. Don't steal other people's stories. It's ok to tell someone else's story if you ask their permission (if you know them personally) or give attribution. For example, I might tell a story I read in a book and say something like, "I recently read about a similar situation in [book title] by [author]..." If you can't recall the source, you can say, "I once heard a story..." or, "I recently read a case study about..."

4. Don't offend. It's hard to persuade or engage people if they are offended. Don't make fun of anyone other than yourself (and don't overdo that). Know your audience well enough you don't accidentally offend them

5. Ditch the back story. Provide just enough background to make the story relevant or understandable. Get to the conflict or problem as quickly as possible. Otherwise, you will likely bore people.

6. Use a storytelling format that leaves your listeners leaning forward. A story is usually only interesting if there is CONFLICT. Conflict can be external (conflict with another person, a circumstance, or society) or internal (a struggle of the mind).

a. Standard hero's journey format:

(Main character) is in (circumstance/setting) and needs to (goal) but faces (obstacles/opponents) when (climax/conflict at a high point) until (resolution—obstacle or opponents are overcome).

Here's a personal story I often use to convey how behaviors must be in line with values if you are a person of integrity:

"Many years ago, when my children were small, I *(main character)* dropped my daughter off at a home-based preschool *(setting/goal)* and backed right into the preschool teacher's truck. I got out and assessed the damage. There was no damage to my van, but there was a foot-long dent in the teacher's truck—more than $500 in damage. Ouch! Five hundred dollars was a big deal to me, as my family was struggling financially *(obstacle-circumstance causing internal struggle)*. Nobody saw me back into the truck. If I just left, no one would know it was me. Should I say something, or should I keep quiet?

"I realized it was a question of integrity *(conflict at a high point)*. Would my behavior be in line with my values?

"After I hit the preschool teacher's car, I had a choice. If I had simply left, my behavior would not have aligned with my values. I valued honesty. I valued taking responsibility for one's actions. So, I rang the doorbell. When the preschool teacher answered, I delivered the news, 'I'm so sorry, I just backed into your truck. I'll pay for the damage.' Cost: $675. Intact integrity: priceless!" *(resolution)*.

b. C.A.R.: Challenge-Action-Result

While the standard hero's journey format contains the essential story elements, it's easier to remember to tell a story using the C.A.R. format in an impromptu situation. C.A.R. stands for **C**hallenge, **A**ction, **R**esult.

> **C**hallenge: Talk about the problem
>
> **A**ction: Talk about what action you or your team took
>
> **R**esult: Talk about the result (or what you learned)

Here's an example of a business story using CAR

Challenge: Several years ago, a company hired me to work with one of their senior technical experts, Michael, on an upcoming conference presentation. One of their biggest concerns was that Michael's excessive use of *ums* would reflect poorly on the company. Michael was more concerned that his excessive ums would damage his credibility as an expert.

Action: I recorded him practicing his 3-minute speech introduction and then had him watch the recording. After watching it, he turned to me and said, "That was awful!" He had 30 ums in 3 minutes, a high rate of ums. I then had him repeat his speech introduction, but with one small difference. Every time he said, "um," I would hit an empty can of Coke. At first, Michael would cringe when I hit the can, but soon, he paused instead of saying, "um." Then I had him give his introduction a third time, again recording it, but without hitting the can.

Result: He had only three ums in 3 minutes. Success! A few ums are not that noticeable. Two weeks later, I received an email from Michael. His presentation was a success. For the first time ever, people in the audience came up to him and told him how much they appreciated the information.

c. A more advanced format: Then-Now-How format

Would you like a subtle strategy to get your prospective clients, customers, management, or even prospective employers leaning forward, wanting to hear how you can help them?

Try using a story with the Then-Now-How format. I first learned this story format from Craig Valentine, a top business speaker and a Toastmasters World Champion of Public Speaking.

The secret to the power of the Then-Now-How story format lies in the order in which you present the points. It is a non-linear way to tell a story in which you show the solution to the problem before explaining how it was solved.

It's like when you see weight loss products or services advertised. You see a "before" (then) picture and an "after" (now) picture. You want to know how the dramatic change was achieved, so your curiosity pulls you into the advertisement to find out how they did it.

First, you talk about a "then" situation that focuses on what the problem was.

Second, you talk about the "now" situation that focuses on the positive result or benefits.

Third, you tell "how." By delaying "how" until after the "now," you get people leaning forward and wanting to hear the how.

If I rearrange the order of the previous story, it would be:

Then: Several years ago, a company hired me to work with one of their senior technical experts, Michael, on an upcoming conference presentation. One of their biggest concerns was that Michael's excessive use of ums would reflect poorly on the company. Michael was more concerned that his excessive ums would damage his credibility as an expert.

I recorded him practicing his 3-minute speech introduction and then had him watch the recording. After watching it, he turned to me and said, "That was awful!" He had 30 ums in 3 minutes, a high rate of ums.

Now: Fast-forward 10 minutes. Michael had just given his introduction again, but this time with only 3 ums in

3 minutes. Success! A few ums are not that noticeable. And two weeks later, I received an email from Robert. His presentation had been a success. For the first time ever, people in the audience came up to him and told him how much they appreciated the information.

How: How did Michael so drastically reduce his ums in such a short time? It involved a pen, a Coke can, and making an annoying sound. After the first 3-minute practice of his introduction, I had him repeat it, but with one critical change. Every time he said "um," I hit my half-drunk Coke can with a pen. At first, every time I hit the can, Michael would cringe and get flustered. But soon, he just paused instead of saying um, to avoid the irritating sound.

Telling the story in this way, out of order, gets the listener leaning forward, wanting to hear more.

Your stories don't have to be big, life-changing stories. It is often better if they are everyday personal or business stories that others can relate to. You can prepare for impromptu storytelling by thinking through a few stories that illustrate key messages based on your values, successes, failures, and changes you have experienced. Start with this idea—what is one of the most important values you have? How did you learn its importance? How does it apply to your profession?

So, what's your story?

#7 AGREE & BUILD ON WHAT OTHERS SAY

Would you like an impromptu speaking technique that makes you look like a team player when you respond? And encourages a spirit of cooperation? If so, take a page from improv, with the "Yes, and..." rule.

The "yes" part of the rule encourages accepting others' contributions, fostering cooperation rather than shutting down communication. The "and..." part of the rule encourages expanding the ideas of others. "Yes, and..." encourages not only collaboration but further contributions by others.

If you've ever watched an improv skit, you have probably seen the "Yes, and..." rule in action. Players create a scene together, often taking suggestions from the audience and building on what the other players say and do. For example, let's say players will be using the improv "Yes, and..." story format, in which each player adds a sentence to a story, starting the sentence with

"Yes, and..." The audience might suggest that the scene takes place in a local supermarket. One player starts the story and says, "Oh, look! There's a pink flamingo!" The next player builds on that and might say, "Yes, and it's eating a plate full of nachos." And the person after that might say, "Yes, and the nacho cheese is turning the bird's feathers orange," and so on.

How would the scene go if after the first player said, "Oh, look! There's a pink flamingo!" the second player negated the line offered, saying, "What? Are you blind? There's no pink flamingo. This is a store, not a zoo!"? The first player would likely feel deflated that their suggestion was not accepted, and the scene might die quickly.

And maybe that is needed in some meetings. Sometimes you need to say no or negate an idea to avoid discussing unproductive ideas and keep a meeting on track.

However, there are a lot of good reasons to be open to trying "Yes, and..." It's an excellent tool for brainstorming, divergent thinking, and creating a culture of acceptance, encouraging people to participate. Plus, it allows you to bridge, without being confrontational, between someone else's view or idea and your own.

"Yes, and..." opens communication, acknowledging the validity of what others say while still allowing you to voice your perspective. When you say "Yes," it doesn't mean you agree with everything, but that you can agree with at least part (or in principle). The "...and" allows you to build on an idea, filling in missing components or taking the idea to a new level.

"Yes" affirms the other. And it doesn't have to be the word "Yes." It is about using words that validate or accept what the other person has said.

For example, let's say you are in a meeting to provide a project update. Someone else on the project says to you, "Your estimated completion date for the beta version doesn't seem reasonable, given that we just lost two team members. Don't you think we need to push out the completion date a few weeks?" Your knee-jerk reaction might be to say, bluntly, "No. We don't, because..." Instead, you could validate the concern first (the "Yes" part). "You are right that losing two team members is a challenge." This will make the other person feel like he was heard and that you have a point of agreement. Plus, you are rephrasing part of what he said, which also buys you some time.

Now, you can build on with the "...and" part, providing additional information.

"And we have mitigated that challenge by temporarily allowing overtime for the other team members until a couple of new hires are up-to-speed on the project. It's possible that we may even finish earlier than planned."

Another typical example for using "Yes... and" might be when someone wants something that you can't give, at least not precisely as they would like.

Let's say someone you manage asks you for a pay increase.

The employee might say, "I've been a valuable contributor for more than a year. I'd like a salary increase that reflects my value to the organization."

Knowing that sales are down, you might say, "That's not possible right now." The employee, at a minimum, is disappointed but might also be angry at that response.

Instead, you can validate (say "Yes" to) the employee's statement by first saying, "Yes, you have been a valuable contributor..."

And then you can further explain, "And, that's not possible right now..." (you would probably give a reason or two and invite a conversation to discuss a future raise). You may naturally word the second part instead, "but, that's not possible right now..." Notice the difference? In the second wording, "but" was the connector. Try to avoid turning "Yes, and..." into "Yes, but..." because the "but" shuts down the conversation.

Try using the "Yes, and..." approach to respond in a non-confrontational way.

Respond in this 1-2-3 format:

1. Validate. Open with words of agreement
   - Yes...
   - That's right...
   - You're right...
   - I agree...
   - You are correct...

2. Repeat. Repeat or rephrase the part you agree with.

3. Build on the point of agreement ("...and") with your viewpoint.

#8 HANDLE CRITICISM OR CONFLICT IN-THE-MOMENT

One of the most challenging impromptu speaking situations is dealing with unanticipated conflict or criticism. Handling in-the-moment conflict or criticism is easier if you first unpack how you deal with conflict in general.

What is your usual response to conflict?

- Fight (encourages struggle or competition, sometimes accompanied by eye-rolling; sends the message that "I'm OK, but you're not OK")
- Flight (denial or avoidance; sends the message that "I'm not OK and you're not OK.")
- Freeze (accommodate or smoothing things over; sends the message that "You're OK, but I'm not OK.")
- Face (compromise or collaboration; sends the message that "We're both sort of OK."-compromise or "I'm OK and you're OK."-collaboration)

Depending on the situation, any of the above responses may be appropriate. But in most work situations, facing the conflict in a spirit of collaboration yields the best results. The biggest challenge to getting to the point of collaboration is that conflict usually comes with high emotions that cloud thinking or set up adversarial relationships (people naturally want to respond with fight, flight, or freeze).

If the communication hasn't gone completely off the rails, you can L.E.A.P. into conflict communication.

L.E.A.P. is an acronym developed by Dr. Xavier Amador, author of I'm Right, You're Wrong, Now What?

L.E.A.P. stands for:

Listen Reflectively

Empathize

Agree

Partner

Although the method was first developed to convince people in denial to accept help, it has a broader application in responding to conflict in the moment.

Listen Reflectively: Most people just want to feel heard. Really heard. Don't half-listen while you check your cell phone.

Staying focused on the conversation can be difficult because humans can listen much faster than they can speak. I sometimes will double the playback speed of audiobooks or even fast-forward through some content if I need to get through the book more quickly. It works well for absorbing information quickly, but we can't put our conversation partners on fast-forward.

So, what's the best way to combat mind drift? The cure for this is active, reflective listening: listening with a purpose and not just waiting for your turn to talk. Reflect by paraphrasing, summarizing, or asking questions to clarify.

To ensure you understand the other person (and to buy a little time), follow this two-step clarification procedure:

1. Start with a lead-in phrase, such as:

"So..."

"What I hear you saying is..."

"So, what you're saying is..."

"It sounds like..."

"Are you saying...?"

The first step, the lead-in phrase, doesn't have to be used every time. Often you can simply make a restatement. However, using a lead-in phrase cues the other person you are about to make a clarifying statement or question.

2. Restate facts, feelings, opinions, etc., and encourage additional clarification. When you restate something, ask for clarification or further explanation using a phrase like "Tell me more about that."

Here's an example of a restatement of feelings with a request for clarification:

Jennifer: "LeAnn was late to the weekly meeting again! She is so inconsiderate! It's hard for me not to roll my eyes when I see her come in."

Lynn: "So, it sounds like you are frustrated that LeAnn was late again. Tell me a bit more about that."

Jennifer: "You bet I'm frustrated! It's annoying to have to take the time to recap the meeting for her."

Lynn: "So, what you are saying is that you are frustrated because the recap wastes everyone's time. Is that right?"

Empathize: Empathy is just trying to see things from another person's viewpoint and letting them know you know how they feel. Much of an empathetic response is in your facial expressions and body language (which you can use to subtly mirror them and show responsive feelings to what is being said). And you can show verbal empathy by using phrases such as, "If I were in your shoes, I'd feel the same way..."

If you can empathize with someone, the next step is to find areas of agreement.

Agree: "Yes, and..." the other person. Find common ground. Sometimes it can be as simple as relating to everyday experiences. For example, almost everyone can relate to feeling too busy. You can also agree on the big picture or some common value.

The corollary to "agree" is "don't be disagreeable." Being confrontational is a huge turn-off—you must have some credibility with people before you can be confrontational with them. Strive to be accepting and to move the conversation forward. Use the concept of

"Yes, and..." to accept and build on what the other person says.

Partner: It's not you vs. me. It's we vs. the problem. Focus on solutions.

Applying L.E.A.P. to Dealing with Criticism in-the-moment

a) Avoid getting defensive. Take a breath. Control your facial expression to be neutral. Remember that usually, the criticism isn't a personal attack. It is a sincere concern. And give yourself some grace. Everyone makes mistakes, and no one knows everything. Apply the LEAP concept.

b) Listen & validate the dissenter. "Thank you for your opinion." (or, input, or concern). You want to acknowledge the criticism, perhaps even showing appreciation for an error or possible error.

c) Empathize & and ask clarifying questions (if needed)... Put yourself in their shoes and mention why their concern is important.

Then, if you aren't completely clear on their concern, ask them to explain their position or their reasoning ("Help me understand...").

d) Agree. Find something in common to agree on: "I think we can both agree on ...." At work, this is usually agreeing on the "big picture," or some corporate value, or how to best serve clients or employees. If you agree on the specific criticism, let them know you will address it.

e) Partner. Let them know how you will move forward together. Often, you may need to delay if your response requires additional consideration. "Let me look into this and get back with you by _____(day/time)."

L.E.A.P. into communication in your next conflict situation.

#9 INTERRUPT WHEN NECESSARY

"Don't interrupt! That's rude!" is what I heard growing up. Even now I occasionally interrupt people and jump into a conversation. I blame growing up with an Italian mother. Sometimes I must bite my tongue to force myself not to interrupt.

Interrupting people when they are speaking should be avoided, but sometimes it's necessary. Some possible reasons to interrupt, depending on the circumstances and the corporate culture:

- You have something important to say that can't wait
- You need to gain understanding or clarification
- You need to correct faulty information on a critical matter
- You need to provide timely input
- You need to get a meeting or conversation back on track

- You need to cut off the long-winded talker

It's tricky to navigate the timing for an interruption. You don't want to steamroll over someone and talk over them inconsiderately, yet if you wait too long to interrupt and the moment passes, you and others may suffer. Before you interrupt, unless there is an emergency, make sure your interruption relates to the point being discussed. Then, ask for permission to interrupt:

"Excuse me, may I interrupt for a moment?"

"Excuse me, may I provide some additional information?"

"Excuse me, may I jump in quickly?"

"Excuse me, may I ask a quick question?"

"Excuse me, but I want to make sure I understand…"

Asking if it is O.K. to interrupt shows you are trying to be considerate and that you were indeed listening and not just blurting something out.

You can also use "can" instead of "may" if you are more comfortable with asking, "Can I…? May is the more formal word for asking permission. Can is used to indicate ability, but both can and may can be used. You may use can, or you can use may.

If you are in a culture that very much frowns on interrupting people, you can add in an apology:

"I apologize for interrupting..."

"I'm sorry for interrupting..."

A phrase of apology will soften the interruption and show you understand that interrupting is generally considered rude.

One of the most challenging interruption scenarios is trying to politely cut off the long-winded talker, especially when meeting online or on a phone call. Someone doesn't stop talking, making it hard to exit or hear from others in a meeting. Below are ten tips for taking control of a conversation and bringing it to a close in a professional and (mostly) graceful manner.

1. **Announce your hard stop near the start of the meeting.** "I have a hard stop at 10:30 for another meeting/project."

2. **Interrupt when they pause to breathe.** Eventually, they must take a breath. It will seem more polite if you don't cut them off mid-sentence. Just quickly interrupt when they pause for a breath.

3. **Use respectful language.** Soften the interruption with polite language, such as, "Excuse me... I'm sorry for interrupting."

4. **Make it about YOU, not them.** You DON'T want to say, "Shut up! Just stop talking! Your incessant drivel makes you sound like an incompetent bore." Instead, make it about you (or others), not them. "Excuse me, Kylee, I've got to... finish a big project... get on another call... take my kid to the doctor... etc."

5. **Help them make their point.** Some people aren't just talking; they are thinking out loud, searching for a point. You can assist them by interrupting and asking questions. "Excuse me, Kylee, based on what you've said, what do you recommend?... what is the next step... are you saying (the point you think they are making)?"

6. **Appeal to inclusion/diversity.** If there are more than two people in the meeting, and one has been talking for a very long time, interrupt that person to allow someone else to speak. "Excuse me, Kylee, we want to hear from some others as well. John, what do you think?" Also, if there are more than two people in the meeting, it sounds less aggressive to use "we" instead of "I" when saying phrases such as, "We want to hear from others... we need to get a consensus... we want to encourage diverse opinions... we need to wrap up."

7. **Have an agenda and set time limits.** In a large meeting, send out an agenda in advance. You also can set time limits upfront, with everyone limited to 2 minutes at a time for discussion. If that seems too formal, simply get everyone to agree to keep comments short. When someone goes too long, you can interrupt. "Excuse me, Kylee, we need to keep our comments short so that we can get through the agenda."

8. **Get back to the topic.** If the other person has veered off the topic, you can ask them to get

back on topic or use the interruption to change direction. "Excuse me, Kylee, while that is an interesting idea, we need to get back to the main topic…" Or "Kylee, that's a great idea! Let's put a pin in it and get back to the main topic."

9. **Give a gentle warning that time is almost up.** "Excuse me, Kylee, I need to go in just a couple of minutes." And if you can give a reason, such as, "because I have another meeting," that will help ease the almost inevitable abrupt ending. You can also add something about how much you enjoyed talking with them or appreciated their input. You might also confirm any follow-up conversation, email, or action, e.g., "I'll email you the details later today." Then after a couple of minutes, if they are still talking, interrupt them with a final few words and leave the meeting. "I'm so sorry, Kylee, I've got to jump on my next meeting, so I'm logging off now. Have a great rest of your day!" <leave meeting>

10. **Fake an emergency.** When all else fails, and you can't seem to end a conversation, you can

always fake it. Drop something loudly, have a coughing fit, or, if your video is on, look wildly distracted, with a pained expression, and say, "I need to go." <leave meeting>

#10 CONVEY CONFIDENCE WITH YOUR VOICE & BODY LANGUAGE

When you haven't thought too much about what you will say, your non-verbal communication may belie a lack of confidence or may send the wrong message. You want to make sure that your body language aligns with your message. For instance, if you say, "That's an interesting point," but are rolling your eyes or looking away, your nonverbal cues contradict your words. Let's look at how your voice and body language can be improved for impromptu speaking situations.

Voice

Rate, pitch, volume, inflection, fluency, and word choice all contribute to how confident you sound.

Rate

Most people speed up when nervous, which can exacerbate nervousness. When you speak too fast, you give yourself less time to think, and you are more likely to stumble over your words. Your heart rate and breathing can increase, making you feel even more flustered. Instead, slow it down (but not so slow that you put your audience to sleep), pause between thoughts, and come across as calm and confident.

Pitch

People view speakers with lower speaking voices as having more confidence and authority. You don't want to sound unnatural, as speaking unnaturally high or low can sound insincere. Try to find your "perfect pitch" by relaxing your throat, closing your lips, and humming. Then, use your humming tone as your baseline vocal pitch.

Volume

While soft tones can be attention-getting when used purposefully, speaking softly sounds timid, like you are afraid to speak up and be heard. You don't want to yell, but <u>research</u> (Van Zant & Berger, 2020) has shown that speaking a little louder than you normally would generally is more persuasive.

Inflection

Avoid upspeak (or uptalk) to sound confident. Upspeak is the tendency to have a rising intonation at the end of sentences so statements sound like questions, making the person sound uncertain. "I'm with the HR department?" sounds like the person isn't sure they are with the HR department. To improve, practice statements ending on a downward inflection.

Fluency

Fluency is speaking with a smooth continuity and without excessive disfluencies such as "uh" or "um" or filler words, such as "like" or "you know." Your fluency should improve when you come to a meeting prepared and when you have an approach to answering a question. Replace "uh" and "um" or other filler words with a pause. Just. Be. Silent.

Word Choice

Avoid words or phrases that minimize the power of your statements. The biggest offender is the word "just" in phrases such as, "I just wanted to say... " or, "I just wanted to add..." Using "just" this way makes you sound less confident and almost apologetic, Instead, directly make your statement.

Body language

Body language includes your use of space, posture, gestures, facial expressions, eye movements, and general appearance. Different cultures have different norms for personal space, gestures, facial expressions, and eye contact. Do your homework if you are speaking cross-culturally.

Use of space

In a nonverbal context, your use of space means how much space you take up and the distance between you and others. Being too far away or much lower than others can make you look weak. Being too close or hovering too much above others can make you look intimidating. Try to be at the same height as others, which may mean adjusting your seat if seated at a meeting.

This is also true for virtual meetings. Sitting (or standing, if you have a standing desk) about an arm's length away from your camera, with your camera at eye level, is a good use of space. Much further away than that, you look too small; much closer, you look like you are invading personal space.

Use of space also includes how much space you physically take up. More space looks more confident (if not overdone). You don't want to crowd out others, but you deserve as much space as others. Go ahead, uncross your arms, and rest them on the meeting table so you can make expansive gestures with your hands, letting you use even more space when you speak. Take a slightly wider stance with your feet when standing.

Posture

You can take up more space with a tall, confident posture, whether standing or sitting. A study in Health Psychology (Nair et. al., 2015) found that participants seated in an upright posture during a speech had higher self-esteem and a better mood than those in a slumped posture. Whether standing or sitting, you can imagine that you are like a puppet on a string, with the string gently pulling your head up toward the ceiling, elongating your spine. And then, leaning in just a little, bend slightly at the waist. Leaning in very slightly reduces the space between you and others and indicates interest.

With all the time most people spend on their devices, it's hard to break a hunched-posture habit. Another way to improve your posture is to think "head over shoulders" to align your head with your shoulders instead of slouching. For online meetings, elevate your laptop or external camera so you have to sit tall to look into the lens at eye level. Keep your head and chin up. Confident people look up, not down at the table or the floor.

Gestures

Let your hands speak! Not only can gestures enhance meaning for listeners, but several studies (Clough & Duff, 2020) have also shown that using gestures may facilitate word retrieval and fluency when people speak. Reduce that "tip of the tongue" feeling of knowing but not quite remembering something.

Generally, you want your hands visible, at least in in-person meetings. Keep your hands out of your pockets.

Some gestures enhance your confident appearance:

- Broad, smooth movements show calm composure
- Palm up gestures show openness
- Descriptive gestures to indicate size, shape, a count, or comparison
- Steepling (holding your fingers together with your palms separated)

Other gestures detract from a confident appearance:

- Fidgeting or tapping
- Touching your neck or face
- Playing with hair or jewelry
- Wringing your hands

Facial expressions

Facial expressions can reflect your thoughts. And that's not always a good thing. Let's say you are asked an unexpected question in a meeting, one you think is a stupid question. If your facial expressions reveal your thoughts, you might shake your head, roll your eyes and sneer. Even if the question was ill-informed, your facial expression was not a good look. Or maybe the unexpected question was one you should have prepared for but didn't. You might raise your eyebrows and grimace. Also, not a good look. It is preferable to control your facial expressions in most professional settings while processing your response. While in listening mode at a meeting, aim for a relaxed, pleasant expression with the corners of your mouth slightly up as default expression, unless the topic is sad or disturbing. For a serious topic, just drop the smile to look serious, but without frowning. However, if the topic is a positive one you are passionate about, smile warmly to engage with others as you speak.

Eye contact

My six-year-old self can still hear my mother's voice saying, "Look at me when I'm talking to you!" My mother taught me that making eye contact was important. She was right. Appropriate eye contact can show respect and confidence. Making almost no eye contact may indicate low self-esteem, unpreparedness, dislike, disinterest, or dishonesty. Staring or making prolonged intense eye contact may indicate aggressiveness (it can greatly depend on your expression).

Show confident eye contact by first establishing eye contact before you speak. Then, gaze into the eyes (or one eye, or even near the eyes) of the other person, holding your gaze for 3-5 seconds before briefly breaking off or looking at another person. In online meetings, that means looking directly into the camera lens when speaking, treating the camera lens as the eyes of your conversation partner.

CONCLUSION

Will you be prepared to rise to the occasion, to speak, when given the opportunity?

I hope your answer is "yes."

Or at least that you want it to be "yes."

Your opportunity may be on the job, in your business, or for a cause you care about when you speak from the heart and inspire others to action.

Improving your impromptu speaking skills won't happen if you only read this book. Knowledge gives you the power to change, but without action, knowledge is meaningless. You can reinforce your knowledge and practice impromptu speaking skills in many ways, including:

- Pick a strategy—discuss & practice with others
- Pick a strategy—teach it to your children or others
- Start with ONE impromptu framework to practice at home and work (probably P.R.E.P.)

- Consider taking an improv class or joining a Toastmasters club

The 10 Strategies for Impromptu Speaking:

#1 Anticipate Impromptu Speaking Situations

#2 Know 3 Things: Your Audience, Yourself & Your Stuff

#3 Be Present: Pay Attention & Listen Actively

#4 Buy Time When Called on Unexpectedly

#5 Use Impromptu Speaking Frameworks

#6 Tell a Relevant Story

#7 Agree & Build on What Others Say

#8 Handle Criticism or Conflict In-the-Moment

#9 Interrupt When Necessary

#10 Convey Confidence with Your Voice & Body Language

By using the ten strategies for impromptu speaking, you can change others' thinking, your professional life, and your world.

Yes, you can "Think on Your Feet without Tripping Over Your Tongue!"

REFERENCES

Clough, S., & Duff, M. C. (2020). The Role of Gesture in Communication and Cognition: Implications for Understanding and Treating Neurogenic Communication Disorders. *Frontiers in human neuroscience, 14,* 323. https://doi.org/10.3389/fnhum.2020.00323

Nair, S., Sagar, M., Sollers, J., 3rd, Consedine, N., & Broadbent, E. (2015). Do slumped and upright postures affect stress responses? A randomized trial. *Health psychology : official journal of the Division of Health Psychology, American Psychological Association, 34*(6), 632–641. https://doi.org/10.1037/hea0000146

Van Zant, A. B., & Berger, J. (2020). How the voice persuades. *Journal of personality and social psychology, 118*(4), 661–682. https://doi.org/10.1037/pspi0000193

APPENDIX A: IMPROMPTU TOPICS

Below are 36 general topics to practice with family and friends (Use P.R.E.P. or Point/Story/Lesson, or another framework. Speak for 45 seconds – 2 minutes. Imagine tagging the question "And why?" at the end of these topics.)

1. What is your dream vacation?
2. What is the best advice you have ever received?
3. If you could go back in time and give your 12-year-old self advice, what would it be?
4. What is the strangest thing you believed as a child?
5. As a child, what did you want to be when you grew up?
6. What life lesson did you learn the hard way?
7. If you could give new parents your top tip, what would it be?
8. What was the best thing about the worst job you ever had?

9. What was your first job?
10. Who do you admire the most?
11. Which season do you like best?
12. What do you need more of in your life?
13. What do you need less of in your life?
14. What do you imagine yourself doing in 10 years?
15. What is your favorite holiday (or family tradition)?
16. If you could have a conversation with anyone, dead or alive, who would it be?
17. If you could know the future, would you want to?
18. What is one of your top pet peeves?
19. What does the word "success" mean to you?
20. What makes you a good friend? (Or mother, father, sister, coworker, boss, etc.)
21. What do you wish you had learned that you haven't learned (yet)?
22. What is something new you want to try?
23. What is something you've tried but would never do again?
24. What is the best pet to own?

25. If you could bring back a fashion trend, what would it be?
26. What is one of your top values, and how did you learn it?
27. What is a challenge you have overcome?
28. What is the most difficult thing you have ever done?
29. What are you thankful for?
30. What would you do differently if no one judged you (or knew you couldn't fail)?
31. What is the best/worst movie you ever watched?
32. If you could be any animal for a day, what would you choose?
33. What makes you happy?
34. If you were the leader of your country, what would you do first?
35. What's something people might be surprised to know about you?
36. Milk chocolate or dark chocolate?

APPENDIX B: TIPS FOR SPECIFIC IMPROMPTU SITUATIONS

You can and should prepare for these situations, but sometimes you run out of time and need a simple game plan. Entire books could be (and have been) written on most of the topics below.

Crisis Communications

You may be able to anticipate potential crises by asking yourself (and brainstorming with others), "What if something goes wrong?" And then create a crisis communication plan for areas of high negative impact. When a crisis occurs, respond quickly to get in front of the situation and control the narrative by putting the crisis in the context you want it seen in yet being as transparent as possible. The truth will come out, so you might as well be upfront. You can always give yourself a little "breathing space" with statements, such as "We are monitoring the situation and will post updates on our website." Avoid blaming others at the outset (you can do that later). Instead, focus on the victims, and provide information and action to help them. "Our highest priority is the health and safety of our customers."

Farewell Speeches

In everyone's career, often more than once, you will leave a company or team. You might be promoted, relocated, retiring, or moving on to another company. Typically, you will make a short farewell speech on your last day or at a going-away party. You can start in many ways, with a quote or with a funny anecdote about something that happened at work. Talk about the company and your coworkers with praise, mentioning your favorite experiences and what you have gained. You can conclude by describing mixed emotions about leaving, being excited about what is ahead but sad about leaving your coworkers. End with a thank you.

Funeral Speeches/Memorials (Eulogy)

When stepping up to eulogize someone, keep your words positive (this is not the time to discuss the cause of death or old hurts). Let people know what your relationship is with the deceased. Share the positive memories you have of the person, telling one or more favorite stories that highlight the kind of person they were. If the person made a difference in your life, tell the story of how that came to be.

Humorous Moments

People will relax and engage if you can interject relevant, non-offensive impromptu humor into conversations and presentations, especially when something doesn't go as planned. The two easiest ways to do that are to either use self-deprecating humor (making fun of yourself) or observational humor (making fun of the situation or something everyone can observe). Don't make fun of others, and don't be too hard on yourself, or people will cringe.

Impromptu Meetings

Sometimes an urgent situation, an opportunity, or a challenge, requires an impromptu meeting. These meetings are often best handled online, with webcams on to increase focus and collaboration. Invited attendees should include those with a specific role, perspective, or information. Let attendees know at the start what the desired outcome is. Explain the situation, get information and perspectives by inviting people, round-robin style to chime in, or call on specific individuals.

Job Interviews

To prepare for a job interview, comb through your credentials/resume and the job description, looking for key skills and experience you can turn into questions that you practice answering, using either P.R.E.P. or S.T.A.R. (for behavioral interview questions). There are also numerous sites online with general practice questions. Role-play questions with a friend or family member, if possible. Occasionally, you may have an impromptu interview when you meet someone who is hiring for a job, or you get a surprise call from a recruiter. Be friendly yet professional. Focus on your accomplishments.

Media Interviews

You may be asked to answer questions in an impromptu media interview. Depending on the situation, know what you can and cannot mention. Know why you are being interviewed. Stick to key, relevant messages. Don't lie or make anything up.

Consider using P.R.E.P. (Point, Reason, Example, Point) as a primary way to answer questions.

Opinion

Someone has asked you your opinion. If you feel that the situation warrants an opinion and you have the basis for making an informed opinion, consider first asking more questions about the situation or the issue. Listen closely and pay attention to the person's attitude requesting your opinion, so you can avoid triggering a defensive or aggressive response. State your opinion so it leaves room for alternate interpretations of the facts (or lets it be known that you might not have all the facts). Start with a lead-in phrase such as, "Based on what I know..." Or "From my point of view..." Or "Given what I have seen/experienced..." Then, you can use the P.R.E.P. approach to plainly state your opinion, backing it up with logic and evidence or examples.

Networking Introduction

You are at a networking meeting and are invited to introduce yourself (you should expect that, right?). Start with your name, your business name (or company/department), and a short "bumper sticker" length sentence (ideally, fewer than 15 words) that answers three questions: 1. What do you do? 2. Whom do you do it for? 3. How do they benefit? Here's an example of what I might use. "I'm Diane Windingland with Virtual Speech Coach. I coach and train subject matter experts to speak with clarity and confidence." Then, if you have more time, you could provide an example or a client success story, ending again with your name and business.

Panel Q&A

If you are the panel moderator, you can solicit questions in advance or have people submit questions at the meeting but before the panel session (if you are in an online meeting, the audience can send questions to you in the chat). You can then preview the questions and weed out the confusing or inappropriate ones. If you are responding to questions as part of a panel, one of the more challenging situations is when the same question is asked of each panel member, and you are the last one to answer. If you feel that the other panelists will mention all the great ideas before your turn, you can always provide a funny or surprising viewpoint. Or you can showcase your expertise by digging deeper into the question using a phrase such as, "Let's look at the underlying question..." Or "Let's answer the question behind that question..."

Podcast Interviews

So, you are going to be a guest on a podcast! There is much you can do to prepare, such as actually listening to the podcast to get a feel for the format and the host and asking the host how you can prepare (the host may suggest some topics/questions). Don't have a script in front of you with your answers written out (bullet points with key ideas are OK). Most podcasts are a conversational back and forth banter, with the host asking follow-up questions to what was just said. Go with the flow!

Political Speeches/Debate

Know your key platform points and build on those points in response to questions and debates. Use your key points as sound bites that are the core message of your speech. People will remember the short, catchy soundbite. Support your points with relevant stories and easy-to-understand statistics, drawing upon figures and ideas from the past that appeal to the audience. Present a positive vision of the future. Ideally, you will know your opponents' positions and frame your points as the better choice.

Small Talk

In social situations, networking, and conversation before events, you can sound like a conversational genius when you employ techniques to get others talking. A general approach is to make a positive comment about something you have in common (the food being served, the event). Or you can comment on something you observe. Then, ask a related question, listen to the answer, and respond positively to their answer, ideally paraphrasing some aspect of what they just said. You can then extend the topic with your own experience or ideas or pivot to another related topic. Try this CALREP approach:

- Comment—make a positive comment on something in common or that you observe
- Ask—ask a related question
- Listen—listen carefully
- Respond—respond positively
- Extend—extend the topic with your own experience or ideas, or

- Pivot—pivot to a related topic

Toasts

Toasts are a fun way to celebrate at weddings, dinner parties, anniversaries, and other special events. While it is best to prepare in advance for a toast, don't let a lack of preparation hold you back from giving the gift of a toast to someone you care about. Here is one format:

Start with a hook (don't start with the boring information of how long you have known the person or your relationship). The hook will probably be the tease to a fun or heart-warming story. For example, "John is someone you can always count on. I first learned that when we were kids."

Next, give just a little background on why you are giving the toast and your relationship with the person. Feel free to punch it up to make it fun. You could say, "John is my older brother and when we were kids, I was his tormentor…"

Then give the short story you teased with the hook in the introduction. "I didn't torment him on purpose, but one day… and that's how I knew my big brother was someone I could always count on."

Finally, raise your glass in a Toast and say something like, "Cheers!" or "Let's raise our glasses to toast John, the man we can always count on, and wish him well!"

Voice Mail

Most people hate listening to voice mail almost as much as people hate leaving voice mail, but if you must leave a voice mail, make it brief (under 30-45 seconds), start with your name, company (if applicable), and phone number (say it twice) and then, briefly explain why you want them to call you. Keep it to one or two points.

Wedding Speeches/Toasts

The easiest structure for a wedding speech or toast is Past/Present/Future.

Past: During the wedding, you will probably recall a happy or funny situation you shared with the bride and/or groom. You can open with this story (include your name and how you know the bride and/or groom). "I'm Joe Smith, the brother of the groom, Jim. I remember when Jim told me he wanted to marry a woman who loved him the way he was. I wasn't so sure about that because Jim is such a klutz. One time he even managed to trip over his own feet and fall headfirst onto a cowpie." (Depending on the story, you could add more detail).

Present: Pay attention during the wedding for something that can tie into your previous story. You are looking for a special moment at the wedding with something in common with your story from the past. Use a linking phrase, such as, "I was reminded of that story today..." As in, "I was reminded of that story today when Jim tripped on the way up to the altar. At least this time, he fell into the arms of his bride. Clearly, Janice loves him and his klutzy ways."

Future: Tie in the story to a happy future. (Raise your glass in a toast) "Here's to a long, happy, and mostly accident-free marriage! Cheers!"

ABOUT THE AUTHOR

Diane Windingland is the author of several books on communication skills and the owner of Virtual Speech Coach. Originally trained as an engineer, she spent years having awkward communication skills. Since 2011 she has spoken for organizations that want to help their people have better, more profitable conversations and presentations. She also coaches subject matter experts on how to present with clarity and confidence, shaping what they know into presentations that engage and get results. Diane lives with her husband, Kim, in Minnesota, land of 10,000 lakes and 10 billion mosquitos.

www.VirtualSpeechCoach.com

Other books by Diane Windingland (available on Amazon):

100 Tips & Tricks to Appear Confident in Presentations: Public Speaking Success in 5 Minutes or Less

Section 1: How You Prepare to be Confident

Section 2: How You are Seen

Section 3: How You are Heard

Section 4: How You Answer Questions

Section 5: How You Present Virtually

Cat Got Your Tongue?: Powerful Public Speaking Skills & Presentation Structures for Confident Communication or, How to Create the Purrfect Speech

- MANAGE the fear of public speaking
- Learn how to PRACTICE without memorizing
- Discover powerful speech STRUCTURES
- Learn time-tested RHETORICAL DEVICES
- "Find the Funny" and effectively use HUMOR
- Develop DYNAMIC Openings and closings
- Create engaging STORIES
- Learn key DELIVERY techniques

www.ingramcontent.com/pod-product-compliance
Lightning Source LLC
Chambersburg PA
CBHW071515220526
45472CB00003B/1032